Still
will you^ love me *if*
i love him
her ?

Will You Still Love Me if I Love Her?

Lauren Elizabeth Taylor

laureneltaylor
twitter/instagram

Family,

I barely ever talk to you
about my private life.
Every time my mouth
turns dry. Standby,
truth will spill before I die,
laid to rest or crucified.

Trigger Warnings

Homophobia
Self-harm

Contents

MY FIRST KISS

My first kiss was a girl
with soft, full lips.
She laughed when mine
grazed her neck,
followed a path down
to her collar bone.
My hand gripped
hers, sweaty and shaking,
as I rolled my hips.

The fabric of her top was
velvet, maroon.
I'll never know what
her skin feels like
but I imagine it to be
as smooth as her move
away from me
when her mother
walked in the room.

My 'first kiss' was a boy
with soft, full lips.
He leant over
the handlebars of his bike

and pressed his
against mine,
I liked it
- the beginning of a
potential relationship.

We did not date long
enough to love
but my friends
still gushed,
they were happy for me.
I'd found someone,
they said, 'finally,'
because she was a secret
and he didn't have to be.

ATTRACTION

They walk around her like tourists.
A beauty so rare, foreign to all,
reclaimed by strangers.
She smiles for their unblinking eyes.
Film exposed, the impression pale,
locked inside their minds.
It is a confidence undocumented.
No museum holds her frame,
no database has her name.
Perfection, lingers on my lips.
Stopping tracks, taking breaths,
melting stone-cold hearts.
I want to be her.

Her lips, her cheeks, her hair
comprise every colour on the spectrum,
pour awe down throats like honey,
rouse dust in the depths of empty ribcages.
Deserving of a spotlight, God must have
made the sun just for her. She stands,
a silhouette amongst shadows.
She is so much, so much so
that she may be an illusion, a dream,
a fever high fantasy.

Attraction. I am a tourist too.
No, I cannot think that way.
'You want me,' her caption reads.
'No. I want *to be* you.'
I want *to be* you.
I want *to be* you. The words are as
preprogrammed as breathing,
but they burn my throat. I know.
Give my heart the beating it deserves.
Curves and contours stain my eyelids,
beauty bleeds outside the lines,
her memory will outlive clarity.
I am a tourist longing to find a home
in the landscape I deny myself visitation.

And as they walk around her, I run away.

FRAUD

Shame rests on my chest heavier than his head.
How I tire of his warmth — it covers my exterior
but does not seep through to my bones.
I shiver inside my skin.

I never thought it would hurt this much to not be in
love. To crawl into the 3am cold, crisp sheets and
settle two feet away from where I should be.
We are worlds apart.

He is wonderful and worthy of so much more than I
can give. Guilt sickens my stomach with each
insatiable kiss. Why would 'I love you' mean more
from a woman's lips?

HAPPY HOUR

She knows. It is in her smirk. And smuggled into half-kept secrets, whisky whispers, and promises of never. *Kiss me*, she insists, her face so close to mine that I can smell the beer on her breath. So I kiss her, my tequila tongue yearning to taste hers. Gentle and soft, at first. She pulls away, with giggles spilling from wet, bottle-pursed lips. *I love you*, she says. *You're my best friend.* (The alcohol or me?) She tires of our games and I am the only one left playing. Drunken, dizzy, unable to win, unable to lose. Stuck in limbo, the legacy she leaves behind.

FRESH

I remember the first time
I smelt shampoo waft
from a girl's hair.
     Strawberries.
I paused and wondered
what it would be like
to run my fingers through
the soft strands,
to smell the
strawberries
on my skin too.

I remember the first time
I tasted the edge of a
razor, given by her.
     Strawberries.
I fell in more ways
than one, far darker
than I expected,
and while those
strawberries
did not stain my skin,
the cuts did.

Distance

Are the stars as jealous of the sun as
        I am when   his arms
                        warm your body?

If we were the same distance away could you pick
him over
           me?

Is proximity what makes him? He is close and
        I am   so far.
          My heart hurts.

I may die at anytime, and you will still
        see me
                    standing there,

I will always look the same to you.   Do I look
the same
                as all the others?

Will your eyes search for me at night?
                I am there.
         Can you see me?

                    Come-

HERE I AM

I don't want to die without her.
I have not yet started living.
How does one begin to breathe
when they have been conditioned
to deny their heart its beating
and their eyes ungoverned vision?
Perhaps, I have spent too long
honouring tradition.

I have kept myself censored.
I owe myself forgiveness.
Through all these years of boys and men,
some sweet, some kind, some vicious,
not one has satisfied my soul,
my truth still has no witness.
It seems I have spent too long
living a life fictitious.

HOLD ME

I hope you find me before I crumble.

Think me beautiful despite my battle scars, swollen eyes, and war-torn soul. Do not think me damaged goods, *don't you dare*. I have not sacrificed myself for anything less than love. And love does not exist without respect and hold me in the night,
please hold me.

Mixed Fabric

Source me from the surface
Shallow, the fibre of my being
Immerse me in water
Full me, fix me
Am I ready now?

Pick and pluck until my
Flesh and bones are bare
And smooth
Wrap me in linen but
Do not let it touch my skin

My blood cannot soak
It won't stain and stick
Become fixed, I won't
You should not assemble me from
More than one No-

This vein is thicker than the others
You are making me wrong
Unstitch me
Or they will
I just want to look like them

Where is your apology for making me like this?

ROTTEN

I have forgotten the last time
I heard the sound of
her voice.
   Strawberries.
I have dealt with far more
than I should have
but bliss resides
in the absence
of her cadence,
her place in my heart
now vacant.

I have forgotten the last time
I saw a girl and shamed
my admiration.
   Strawberries.
I no longer have
the time to care
who I love more
him or her,
but the smell
of strawberries
still sickens me.

TV

Would you rather watch static?
If indistinct figures moved in flashing
black and white, no gender, no sex
identified, would you still care
who they are and if it is acceptable
for them to love before your eyes?

Would you rather stare at a blank
screen than see an array of colours,
bright and beautiful and - it'll be
your own reflection that you see,
just you, like you, not like me -
black and blue, grey and grey,
saturate the spectrum, won't you?

Will you grip the remote until the
buttons break, break like my heart,
collapsed inside the case? Will the
battery fluid pool under your nails,
spread distaste on your food,
mix with bile on your tongue, like my
name when I announce who I am?

I am like them. The ones who curl
your upper lip, change the channel,
don't look at this shit. There will
be no fags in this house, neither
on the television nor in our living room.
Girls should not kiss girls.
Boys should not kiss boys.
There is no other way than the way
the god you don't believe in
intended there to be.

What will you say? It is a disgrace
that they broadcast queer affection
before watershed, getting their agenda
in the children's heads?
They are everywhere now,
every storyline in every soap,
every comedy, every host,
every question on the quiz shows,
and here still the punchline of every joke.
No one was gay back in my day.
No one is gay in our family.

Please don't try to mute me.

Don't close your eyes, lean back
in your armchair, pretend I am not
there, because I am not the girl
you thought you raised.
This script will not change.
But camera angles do. Can you see me
from a different view? Stop watching
propaganda on the news and look
at your daughter.

Could you, one day, smile
at two brides kissing?
Will you play my wedding tape
on your television?

This Is My Kingdom

For the first time, I found myself
dancing in a rain of glass,
making dust of my own walls.
Fear forgotten, shame erased,
allowing myself to indulge.
This is my freedom from the dark,
this is not my downfall.
Silence severed, pride in possession,
banishing who I once was.
I have waited long enough.
Watch me reign.

I Do Not Fancy You

What if I had told them I was gay?
I might not have been invited to
sleepovers, if they knew,
or pulled into toilet cubicles when drunk
or told that I'm loved, because as a lesbian
there must be confusion between
platonic love and romantic love
and god forbid they get too close to me,
I might catch feelings and they might
catch my homosexuality.

Liking girls does not mean that I
ogled your breasts, or imagined what
you looked like naked
during class presentations.
The female changing room, surprisingly,
was not my happy place. I didn't
look around every week before P.E.
and admire the curves on all of your bodies.
I was too busy being self-conscious about my own,
like every girl going through puberty.

I bet you don't assume that every man
fancies you (if you do, fair enough,
this poem is not for you).
Every word I say is not a trick
to get you into my bed,
the only game we're playing is
the one inside your head, and
I am not interested in winning.
You are not a trophy,
straight is not a challenge,
and loving my way is not sinning.

I won't treat you differently because
you are a girl and I like girls,
you are still just my friend.
Our memories need not be soiled with a
sickly sense of deceit, innocence smeared,
because they are no longer memories
with your friend, but with a queer.
I can have friends who are girls and girlfriends
and there is a distinct difference between the two.
Being a woman does not mean I must fancy you.

THIS IS NOT NEW TO ME

This is not new to me. Stop projecting your
                            confusion and uncertainty.
                            Questioning
                     my understanding of
               my own sexuality.
               Will repetition convince
                     you of my
                            validity?
This is not new to me. I refuse to be the face of
                            your hypocrisy.
                     I am not in need of saving,
                            I don't care
                     if you disagree.
                     I just need you
                            to care enough
               to listen to me.
This is not new to me. And educating you is not
                            my responsibility.
               I do not owe you answers.
               Back off.
                     Respect my privacy.
                            You preach it
                     but you do not
                     practise equality.
This is not new to me. So I won't hold my breath
                            for your apology.

FOR YOU

I know not to settle.

    When the time comes, I will crawl into your warm, protective arms and fall asleep to a goodnight kiss, and I will know reality as sweeter than dreams.

    Many moons may pass until then

                but I am patient.

UNGODLY

I'm being chased by the devil,
he thinks I'm something I'm not.
They're convinced that I'm evil
because of who I love
so they've set him upon me,
they say the sinful should rot.
He's following, he's closer, he's confused
because I'm not what he thought.
I am not evil, anymore than they are.

I'm being chased by the devil
but I'm being chased towards God.
He's standing there with open arms
because love is love.
Hateful actions inspired by faith —
they say they did it in His name.
They're loyal, they're faithful, they're confused
because love is good, and hate is the sin,
and if the devil sees that, so should they.

TRACTION

All these words,
let them weigh on your head
until they sink through bone and
slither from your mouth as easy
as your daughter's name.

The world is changing, Father.
And it will not wait for you.

Acknowledgements

Thank you to the publications who gave my voice a home. 'Attraction' and an earlier version of 'Fraud' were first published by Royal Rose Magazine in December 2018. 'TV' was first published in Issue 3 of Constellate Literary Journal in January 2019.

About the poet

Lauren is a writer and poet, mainly of LGBTQ+ and mental health themed works, from Derbyshire, England. She has a Master of Arts in publishing and dreams of owning her own press. When she isn't consumed by words, Lauren plays the piano and watches horror films with her grandparents.

Other works
How Will I Sound When My Voice Returns?

Printed in Great Britain
by Amazon

86788360R00021